Original title:
When We Were Whole

Copyright © 2024 Swan Charm
All rights reserved.

Author: Sebastian Sarapuu
ISBN HARDBACK: 978-9916-79-153-0
ISBN PAPERBACK: 978-9916-79-154-7
ISBN EBOOK: 978-9916-79-155-4

Chronicles of the Sacred Whole

In the stillness, whispers reign,
Echoing praises to the divine,
Hearts unite in the sacred fold,
Stories of grace and mercy told.

Mountains bow and rivers flow,
In unity, our spirits grow,
Through trials faced, in faith we stand,
Guided by a steadfast hand.

The heavens sing a timeless hymn,
Reminding us of the light within,
With every tear and joyful shout,
We carve the path, we walk about.

In silence, prayers rise like smoke,
Binding souls in every cloak,
A tapestry of love we weave,
In the sacred truth, we believe.

Together, we tread the sacred earth,
A celebration of life and rebirth,
With hearts aflame and spirits whole,
We journey forth, one sacred soul.

The Hallowed Lines of Kinship

In golden light, our bonds are drawn,
From dusk till the breaking dawn,
Each line of kinship, truth and grace,
We gather in this sacred space.

The laughter shared, the tears we shed,
Anointed by words we've said,
In the hallowed hall our spirits meet,
With every heartbeat, a rhythm sweet.

Hand in hand, we rise above,
Tethered by a thread of love,
Through trials fierce and tempests bright,
Together we embrace the light.

Echoes of wisdom in gentle sighs,
A mosaic rich beneath the skies,
In every glance, a story spun,
In sacred kinship, we are one.

Through storms that howl and winds that blow,
In faith and love, we choose to grow,
With every step upon this road,
The lines of kinship we uphold.

The Chorus of Our Sacred Past

In every shadow, whispers lay,
The chorus of the past at play,
Voices rise with memories sweet,
A tapestry of tales complete.

Through ancient woods and rivers wide,
In echoes, we find truths abide,
Each note a promise, each breath a song,
In unity, we all belong.

The sky adorned with stars so bright,
Reflects the paths we've walked in light,
Every sorrow, every joy,
In harmony, we shall employ.

From age to age, the stories flow,
Lessons learned as we grow,
In sacred rhythm, hearts will soar,
Together we open every door.

Hand in hand, we sing as one,
In the warmth of the rising sun,
With every heartbeat, we renew,
The chorus of the past rings true.

Ember of Shared Light

In the darkness, embers glow,
A flame of hope we come to know,
With whispers soft and voices clear,
In shared light, we cast out fear.

The circle formed, united strong,
In every heart, we share a song,
Lighting paths with love and grace,
Together we embrace this place.

Through trials faced, we lift our hands,
Creating warmth where silence stands,
Each flicker tells of journeys made,
In every moment, love displayed.

As stars align in the velvet skies,
In unity, our spirit flies,
An ember bright in the sacred night,
Illuminating all with sacred light.

For in our hearts the candle stays,
Guiding us through life's complex maze,
Together kindling, day and night,
The ember of our shared light.

Verses of Blessed Kinship

In the glow of holy light,
Together we stand, hearts bright.
Hand in hand, through trials we tread,
Faith unites, let love be spread.

Through storms that rage and winds that howl,
With sacred whispers, we'll avow.
In shadows deep, our spirits soar,
Bound by grace forevermore.

The bond we forge, a sacred thread,
In prayerful whispers, softly said.
With each word, a vow is cast,
In the heart's embrace, forever last.

Together walking, side by side,
In the journey, our souls confide.
Through valleys low and mountains high,
In kinship's strength, we will not die.

Celebrate this blessed tie,
In unity, we rise and fly.
Heaven's song in harmony,
Together bound in symphony.

The Synthesis of Souls

From seeds of faith, we bloom anew,
In sacred bond, our spirits grew.
In grace we find our deepest care,
A tapestry of love we share.

Through trials faced, we stand aligned,
In every struggle, our hearts entwined.
The essence flows, a river pure,
In this embrace, we shall endure.

With gentle whispers, we seek the dawn,
In light of love, our fears are gone.
Each heartbeat echoes sacred dreams,
In unity, the light redeems.

As stars align in twilight's embrace,
We find our strength, we find our place.
Through every storm, we'll rise above,
In sacred union, we find love.

Together we weave our destinies,
In harmony, with gentle ease.
The synthesis of souls takes flight,
Guided by the eternal light.

Reverent Reflections of Us

In quiet moments, our hearts converse,
In reverence, we feel the universe.
Each breath a prayer, a song divine,
In stillness, we know love's design.

With every glance, a truth revealed,
In sacred spaces, all hearts healed.
Together we dance, a holy rite,
In whispered grace, we find the light.

The mirror of our souls reflects,
The love and hope that each connects.
In shared silence, wisdom flows,
In unity, our spirit grows.

As dawn awakens, blessings shower,
In every moment, we find power.
With gentle smiles, we greet the day,
In reverent joy, we choose to stay.

In each reflection, a story lives,
In humble hearts, the spirit gives.
Bound by grace, forever thus,
In love's embrace, it's clearly us.

Chronicles of the Divine Bound

In the book of life, our tale is spun,
With threads of grace, we've just begun.
In every chapter, joy and strife,
Divine connection shapes our life.

As seasons change, our hearts align,
In sacred trust, our souls entwine.
Through whispered prayers and sacred vows,
We find the strength, the love endows.

In trials faced, our spirits ignite,
Together we rise, in faith's pure light.
The chronicles written in radiant lines,
In love's embrace, our hope entwines.

With every step upon the road,
We carry forth this sacred load.
In the heart's journey, we see it clear,
The divine bound, forever near.

In unity's light, our story thrives,
In every heartbeat, love survives.
Together we ink this sacred bond,
In the chronicles, our spirits respond.

Threads of Celestial Connection

In the silence, whispers rise,
Threads of love in cosmic skies.
Hearts entwined, a sacred song,
Together we are, where we belong.

Woven dreams, in faith we bask,
In the light, we wear our mask.
Guided by a higher call,
In unity, we stand tall.

Every star a prayer cast,
In this realm, our ties hold fast.
Through the distance, grace we seek,
In connection, we find the weak.

In the stillness, we will find,
The threads that bind all humankind.
Sewn with hope, the fabric glows,
A tapestry of love, it flows.

With each breath, we softly weave,
A destiny we dare believe.
In sacred bonds, we tread our path,
With love and faith, we find our wrath.

The Sanctuary of Remembered Wholeness

Nestled deep within the soul,
A sacred space that makes us whole.
In quietude, we find our peace,
Where love abounds, and fears will cease.

In reflection, memories gleam,
A sanctuary, our shared dream.
With every heart that beats as one,
The journey just has begun.

Through trials faced and shadows cast,
The light of grace will hold us fast.
In empathy, we come alive,
In unity, we learn to thrive.

Embrace the past, let it flow,
The lessons learned, the truths we sow.
In every heartbeat, every sigh,
We rise together, you and I.

With open arms, we welcome grace,
In this sanctuary, we find our place.
Hand in hand, with love we stand,
In the wholeness of His plan.

The Reverence of Together

In the presence of the Divine,
Amidst each heartbeat, we align.
Hands held high, we lift our voice,
In reverence, we make our choice.

Together we stand, strong and free,
Bound by love, you and me.
In every challenge, we shall rise,
With faith that leads to brighter skies.

In shadows deep, we find the light,
In every struggle, hearts take flight.
Through gratitude, we pave our way,
In the beauty of shared day.

Let kindness flow, let compassion reign,
In togetherness, we ease the pain.
With open hearts, we intertwine,
A sacred bond, forever shine.

In moments still, in laughter shared,
In reverence, we know we cared.
With every tear and every smile,
Together, we can walk each mile.

Bridge to the Divine Essence

Across the void, a bridge is strung,
A pathway where the lost are sung.
In every heart, a spark ignites,
Connecting souls, in sacred lights.

With every step, we draw so near,
A journey where we shed our fear.
In prayerful whispers, we entwine,
In the essence, we seek and find.

Every moment holds the key,
To the love that sets us free.
Through trials faced, we learn to see,
The bridge that leads to unity.

In silence shared, in laughter bold,
The stories of our hearts unfold.
As we walk this sacred way,
In grace, we trust, come what may.

So let us pave this sacred path,
In the love that conquers wrath.
For in the bridge, we all connect,
To the Divine, our hearts reflect.

Reverberations of Celestial Wholeness

In silence whispers the sacred truth,
Stars align with purpose anew.
Hearts awaken, embrace the grace,
Echoes of love in this sacred space.

Beneath the sky, we find our way,
In unity we rise, come what may.
Hands entwined in gentle prayer,
The cosmos sings, we are aware.

Every breath, a hymn we bear,
In the stillness, divine we share.
Mountains bow to the humbling call,
In reverberations, we are all.

As rivers flow to the ocean's heart,
In every soul, we play our part.
Together we weave the tapestry,
Of celestial wholeness, eternally.

In each moment, the light unfolds,
Transcending time, as truth beholds.
A journey divine, forever blessed,
In harmony's light, we find our rest.

The Light of Our Collective Spirit

In the dawn, a promise blooms,
A beacon bright, dispelling glooms.
Through shadows cast, love's path ignites,
Hearts entwined in sacred rites.

Voices rise like an ancient choir,
Yearning souls, our flames aspire.
Together we stand, forever bound,
In the light of truth, we are found.

From every corner, we gather near,
Echoes of grace, a song sincere.
The warmth of hope, our spirits' guide,
Indivisible, we walk side by side.

Each footprint leaves a mark divine,
Weaving light like a sacred vine.
In every heart, a star takes flight,
Illuminated by love's pure light.

As the universe spins on its axis,
Our collective spirit, nothing lacks.
In unity's embrace, forever endure,
A glimpse of heaven, forever pure.

Ascent Towards the Boundless Unity

In the quiet hills, our spirits soar,
Beyond the sky, to a distant shore.
With every step, we climb in grace,
Towards a light that all embrace.

Mountains whisper of ancient truths,
Within our souls, eternal youth.
Together we rise, hand in hand,
In the journey towards the promised land.

As the sun kisses the horizon wide,
We gather strength, our hearts abide.
In every laugh, in every tear,
Resonates love, forever near.

Together, we weave a vibrant dream,
In the tapestry of love, we gleam.
Each moment a thread, each spirit a spark,
In boundless unity, we leave our mark.

Ascent we take, to heights untold,
With faith as our compass, brave and bold.
In the embrace of grace, we rise anew,
Towards the boundless, a journey true.

Elysian Echoes

In the garden of light we stand,
Voices rise like a gentle breeze.
The whispers of hope stretch forth,
In every heart, a sacred peace.

Angels dance on the golden air,
Their laughter pure as morning dew.
Each note weaves a tapestry,
Of love that binds me and you.

Underneath the celestial dome,
Stars twinkle like dreams from above.
In this realm where souls unite,
We find our eternal love.

The echoes of truth resonate,
Carrying prayers to the Divine.
In moments of doubt, we are still,
In the light, our spirits shine.

Elysian whispers call our name,
Guiding us through the night so clear.
In every heartbeat, we shall find,
The presence of love drawing near.

Fractured Choirs of Grace

In shadows linger hearts forlorn,
The strains of sorrow fill the air.
Yet hope arises through the cracks,
A melody relieving despair.

Voices clash like thunder's roar,
Each lost a note in life's refrain.
Yet in the midst of chaos loud,
Find harmony in every pain.

Through fractured songs, a truth is found,
Grace weaves through the broken seams.
Each tear a note, each sigh a chord,
In life's vast symphony of dreams.

Resonate with sacred trust,
In dissonance, a sweet embrace.
Unified, we rise from dust,
Creating beauty in the space.

For in our hearts, the choirs blend,
A chorus of the lost and found.
Fractured notes converge in praise,
The sacred whispers all around.

Abode of Unity

In the heart where love resides,
All differences gently cease.
In quiet stillness, we abide,
Finding joy in shared release.

Underneath one sheltering sky,
Hand in hand, our spirits soar.
In unity, we learn to fly,
Together, we are evermore.

Voices join in sweet refrain,
Harmonies of each unique song.
In diversity, there is strength,
In our embrace, we all belong.

Let not the walls of fear divide,
For every heart beats in a quest.
In love, we find our true home,
An abode of unity, blessed.

Through troubled waters, we shall tread,
With faith as our steadfast guide.
Together, we shall forge ahead,
In love's sacred unity, abide.

Sanctum of Lost Wholeness

In the depths of silence profound,
We wander through the shattered dreams.
Yet in the stillness of the void,
A whisper calls, or so it seems.

Each fragment tells a tale of grief,
Yet every tear can forge a light.
In this sanctum of lost wholeness,
Hearts are kindled by hope's bright sight.

Come, gather round the broken shards,
With courage, weave a sacred quilt.
From strife emerges gentle grace,
In love's embrace, all wounds are built.

In shadows, find a flickering spark,
A luminous guide through the haze.
For in our hearts, we shall ignite,
A flame that ever brightly plays.

Though lost, we seek to find our way,
In every struggle, seek the whole.
In this sanctum, we discover grace,
Restoring life, reviving soul.

A Prayer for the Sundered Among Us

In silence we gather, hearts so torn,
Seeking refuge in light, from shadows worn.
May healing winds whisper, soft as a dove,
Uniting the broken in the promise of love.

With hands lifted high, we seek to mend,
The bonds of the weary, the hearts we defend.
Let compassion flow like a river divine,
Bringing strength to the lost, a path to align.

In the depths of despair, let hope ignite,
A flame in the darkness, our guiding light.
May grace overflow, as we stand as one,
A tapestry woven, till battles are won.

Through trials we wander, yet never alone,
Each prayer a seed in the hearts we've sown.
For the sundered among us, we lift our voice,
In the hymn of the faithful, we rejoice.

Together we'll rise on faith's tender wings,
In the wake of our struggles, new beginnings brings.
A prayer for the sundered, our mission, our call,
May love, endless love, embrace us all.

The Grace of Intertwined Paths

In the dance of the stars, our fates intertwine,
Each step we take, by design, divine.
Together we wander through shadows and light,
In the grace of our journey, our souls take flight.

With hearts open wide, we walk side by side,
Through valleys of sorrow, our spirits won't hide.
A symphony plays in the whispers of trees,
Reminding us all of the love that can please.

Let kindness be seeds that we scatter with care,
In the soil of the heart, trust blooms everywhere.
As rivers converge, we find strength in the stream,
Woven together, we rise from the dream.

In every encounter, a lesson unfolds,
Stories of courage in futures untold.
May the threads of our lives weave a fabric of grace,
In the circle of time, we find our true place.

With each step forward, our burdens we share,
Echoes of laughter, like breath in the air.
In the grace of intertwined paths, we find,
Unity blossoms, our spirits aligned.

Ceremonies of the Rediscovered Spirit

In twilight's embrace, we gather anew,
With hearts ignited, our spirits break through.
Ceremonies whisper in the hush of the night,
Awakening dreams, guiding us to the light.

Around sacred fires, we share sacred song,
In the pulse of the moment, we feel we belong.
With offerings made, we honor the past,
In the dance of remembrance, our hold is steadfast.

The echoes of laughter, the tears that have flowed,
In the rhythms of life, our true selves bestowed.
Through rituals tender, we reclaim our lost voice,
Finding strength in the silence, we make a choice.

As dawn paints the sky with colors so bold,
We rise from the ashes, our stories retold.
In ceremonies sacred, our spirits take flight,
Rediscovered we stand, basking in the light.

Together as one, let our hearts resonate,
In the love of the sacred, we learn to communicate.
Through ceremonies cherished, united we stand,
In the embrace of the spirit, forever hand in hand.

The Vision of Unity's Bloom

In the garden of hope, where hearts learn to grow,
A vision of unity begins to bestow.
With petals of kindness, we nurture the land,
In the warmth of connection, we reach for each hand.

Each flower a soul, unique in its hue,
Together in beauty, we rise and renew.
In the fragrance of peace, let our voices unite,
In the shadow of doubt, we will be the light.

As seasons may shift, our roots intertwine,
In the soil of compassion, our spirits align.
The vision of love, like a river of dreams,
Flows gently through hearts, igniting new beams.

Through struggles we bloom, resilient and wise,
Facing storms with grace, we embrace the skies.
In the tapestry woven, our colors will gleam,
The vision of unity, a collective dream.

So let us stand tall, in the face of despair,
As we nurture this bond, it strengthens the air.
The vision of unity, forever we seek,
In the garden of love, together we speak.

Chants from the Altered Ground

In the stillness, whispers rise,
Sacred echoes fill the skies.
Voices blend in holy tune,
We gather, hearts like flowers bloom.

From the depths of earth we sing,
Praise to the One who reigns as King.
With every note, our spirits soar,
Chants emerge to seek and implore.

Through trials faced and burdens borne,
We find solace in the morn.
Transcendence flows from ground to crown,
In divine love, we're never down.

A circle formed, united strong,
In fellowship, we sing our song.
Holy presence, guide our way,
Forever within, in night and day.

Beneath the Canopy of Faithfulness

Beneath the branches, green and wide,
Our hopes entwined, our hearts abide.
In sacred shadows, trust we find,
A refuge for our weary mind.

With every rustle, prayers ascend,
Nature speaks, our faithful friend.
Embracing grace, the light breaks through,
In God's embrace, all things renew.

The winds of change may test our will,
Yet under faith, our hearts are still.
Together here, we rise and stand,
Bound united, hand in hand.

In trials faced, in love we cling,
The song of hope, our voices sing.
Beneath this canopy, we rest,
In faithful peace, we are truly blessed.

Light and Shadows in the Sanctuary

In the sanctuary, shadows play,
Softened light begins to sway.
Whispers carry through the air,
Hearts laid open, souls laid bare.

Stained-glass stories painted bright,
Filtering colors, wrong and right.
In holy silence, we confide,
Finding comfort, deep inside.

The flicker dims, yet hope remains,
Illuminating joy through pains.
In the corners, light breaks forth,
Casting warmth, revealing worth.

We gather close, our prayers align,
In every soul, a sacred sign.
Light and shadows intertwine,
In this sanctuary divine.

An Offering to the Fractured Heart

In the stillness of despair,
We gather, lifting wounds with care.
An offering from hearts that ache,
A love that heals, a bond we make.

Through brokenness, we seek His grace,
In every tear, a sacred space.
United by our shared lament,
In faith's embrace, our spirits blend.

From fractured hearts, we rise anew,
With every prayer, our hope imbues.
In gentle words, we find our way,
Each heartbeat echoes, love's display.

Together here, we break the chains,
In sacred circle, joy remains.
An offering of love we share,
For fractured hearts, His healing care.

The Testament of Time

In the stillness of dawn's embrace,
Wisdom whispers in soft grace.
Each moment a thread, finely spun,
We weave our fate 'neath the sun.

Echoes of ancients drift near,
Bearing tales of love and fear.
In the sands of time we trust,
From dust to stars, we rise, we must.

Beneath the weight of the heavens' dome,
We search for truth, a sacred home.
In the heart's chamber, faith ignites,
Guiding lost souls through the nights.

Tears fall like rain, cleanse the earth,
Each trial a lesson, each loss a birth.
In sunsets' glow, our spirits soar,
Embracing change, we seek for more.

With every tick, with every chime,
We gather grace, the test of time.
Hope dances lightly, a fleeting sigh,
In unity's arms, we learn to fly.

Sacred Sojourns of Kin

Hand in hand, we wander the path,
Through valleys of laughter, storms of wrath.
In kinship's bond, a flame so bright,
Illuminates the darkest night.

Stories shared by candlelight,
Whispered prayers take sacred flight.
With hearts entwined, we face the dawn,
Together in faith, forever drawn.

Through trials faced, our spirits grow,
In unity's embrace, love's seed we sow.
Each step we take, a promise made,
In the tapestry of life, our colors played.

In laughter's joy, in sorrow's song,
We find our place, where we belong.
With open arms, we gather near,
In harmony's song, we shed each fear.

Through sacred sojourns, hand in hand,
We walk the earth, we understand.
In the heart's echo, our souls entwine,
Forever bound, in love divine.

Embrace of the Fragmented

In shadows' dance, we find our grace,
Fragments of light in every place.
In brokenness, we learn to heal,
The heart's true song, a sacred deal.

Each scar a story, every tear,
A testament of love held dear.
In the silence thick, we seek the sound,
A symphony where hope is found.

Mending pieces with gentle hands,
Creating beauty from life's demands.
In every crack, the light breaks through,
A canvas of colors, old and new.

With faith as our compass, we shall roam,
Finding solace in every home.
The embrace of the fragmented soul,
A journey sweet, of becoming whole.

In love's embrace, we gather close,
In our imperfections, we find what's most.
We rise like phoenixes, bold and grand,
In unity's power, together we stand.

The Alchemy of Care

From gilded hearts, compassion flows,
A gentle touch, where kindness grows.
In every smile, in every tear,
The alchemy of care is clear.

Beneath the burdens that we bear,
We find the strength in love we share.
In whispered hopes, in tender deeds,
The world transforms, the spirit feeds.

With every act, a healing light,
Guides weary souls from endless night.
In gratitude, we lift each other,
Bound together, sister and brother.

As rivers flow and seasons change,
We nurture life, embrace the strange.
In harmony with nature's rhyme,
We find our way, we conquer time.

Through every shadow, every doubt,
In loving care, we find our route.
The heart's alchemy, pure and deep,
In every promise, love we keep.

The Celestial Reunion

In gardens where the angels tread,
Voices whisper, soft and clear,
Heaven's light, a gentle spread,
Unites our souls, dispels all fear.

Through time and space, we find our way,
In the warmth of love divine,
Each moment shared, a sacred play,
Together in the grand design.

With faith as strong as mountain stone,
We journey forth, hand in hand,
No longer lost, no more alone,
In the glow of the promised land.

The stars above, a guiding force,
They light the paths of those who roam,
In harmony, we chart our course,
In love, we find our true home.

As echoes dance in cosmic song,
We celebrate the bond we share,
In every spirit, we belong,
In each heart, His presence fair.

Illuminated Paths of the Heart

In every heart, a candle burns,
A flickering flame of sacred grace,
As each soul wakes, the spirit yearns,
To seek the light, to find the place.

With open hands, in prayer we stand,
Embracing love, the sweetest art,
Together we weave a gentle strand,
Illuminated paths of the heart.

The river flows, a sacred stream,
Where faith and hope entwine as one,
In quiet moments, we dare to dream,
Awakening joy with every sun.

Each step we take, a leap of faith,
With every breath, He walks beside,
In courage found, we forge our wraith,
In Him, our fears and sorrows bide.

United in the bonds of love,
We rise as one, a vibrant choir,
Ascending to the skies above,
In harmony, we never tire.

Fragments to Fulfillment

In pieces scattered, hearts in pain,
We search for wholeness, for the light,
Through trials faced, in joy and strain,
A journey blessed, both day and night.

Each fragment holds a tale untold,
A glimpse of grace in human plight,
In shadows deep, our spirits bold,
We stitch our dreams with threads of light.

As we embrace our brokenness,
In unity, we learn to heal,
Transcending all, we find the bless,
In every wound, a strength revealed.

Through love's embrace, we find our way,
In every heart, a spark is shown,
From shattered dreams, we rise to play,
In sacred whispers, we are home.

The path may wind, with twists unknown,
Yet with each step, our spirits soar,
In fragments lost, His love is sewn,
In fulfillment found, we seek no more.

Beneath the Veil of the Sacred

Beneath the veil, the mystery lies,
We approach the throne with humble hearts,
In silence profound, the spirit sighs,
With every breath, the journey starts.

The sacred whispers call us near,
A refuge found in peace divine,
In shadows cast, the light is clear,
In every soul, His love will shine.

With open arms, we seek His grace,
In every tear, a purpose flows,
In trusting hearts, the saving place,
Where love abounds and mercy glows.

As faith ignites the darkest night,
Our spirits rise on wings of prayer,
In sacred bonds, we find the light,
Together, we cast away despair.

In every moment, let us dwell,
Beneath the veil where love is found,
In whispered hopes, we know too well,
In sacred silence, our souls are bound.

Harmonies of the Divided Heart

In shadows cast by the heavy soul,
A melody of longing takes its toll.
Each heartbeat echoes in silent prayer,
Yearning for peace in the world's cold glare.

The whispers of faith in the dusky night,
Guide the fragmented towards the light.
With every tear, a lesson to learn,
In fractures deep, the spirit shall burn.

Among the stars, a clash of dreams,
Yet in the chaos, hope gently gleams.
The heart's divisions can mend, align,
Creating a symphony, pure and divine.

Let every sorrow be a stepping stone,
In every fissure, a truth to be known.
United in love, though set apart,
Harmony reigns in the divided heart.

And from the depth of despairing strife,
Blooms the grace that revives our life.
A song of courage, resilience bright,
Whispers through shadows, toward the light.

Celestial Whispers of Togetherness

In the dawn's embrace, a gentle sound,
Celestial whispers of love abound.
With every breath, we weave our fate,
In unity, hearts become sedate.

Across the skies, where the spirits soar,
Together we rise, connected evermore.
In gratitude's grace, we find our way,
Drawn by the light of a new day.

The universe hums a sacred tune,
As we dance beneath the watchful moon.
Through trials and joys, hand in hand,
The bond of togetherness does withstand.

In the stillness, the soul convenes,
Filling our hearts with blessed dreams.
Every prayer is a bridge we create,
Reinforcing the love that won't abate.

Empathy flows like a river wide,
With currents of kindness forever tied.
In the tapestry of life, we share and learn,
Celestial whispers beckon our return.

Resplendent Shards of Being

In the quiet glow of the evening star,
Resplendent shards reflect who we are.
Fragmented beauty, a puzzle so bright,
Each piece reveals a spark of light.

We gather the moments, both bitter and sweet,
In the tapestry woven, our spirits meet.
With reverence and grace, we come to see,
The strength in our diversity sets us free.

A mosaic of colors, rich and alive,
In unity's arms, our souls do thrive.
Each shard a story, a life intertwined,
In the essence of love, our paths are aligned.

From shards we rise, not broken but whole,
In every facet, the light of the soul.
Let our hearts resonate with what we glean,
In the dance of existence, true and serene.

For every fracture carries a glow,
In the depths of sorrow, seeds of hope sow.
Resplendent shards, together we sing,
In the harmony of all that life can bring.

Tapestry of Sacred Threads

In the loom of life, our stories entwine,
Threads of purpose in patterns divine.
Each moment a weave, each breath a seam,
Creating a tapestry from a shared dream.

With colors of laughter, with shades of pain,
Together we flourish, together we wane.
The fabric of love, soft yet so strong,
In this sacred journey, we all belong.

Every thread carries a cherished tale,
Of triumphs and trials, our spirits unveil.
Interwoven destinies, crafted with care,
A masterpiece blooming in the open air.

Through storms and calm, we shall persist,
In the dance of the cosmos, we coexist.
Hand in hand, with hearts open wide,
In the tapestry of life, forever we bide.

As sacred threads are cherished and spun,
In the warmth of our union, we become one.
Together we craft, together we mold,
A tapestry rich, where love is retold.

The Psalm of Eternal Kinship

In the quiet of the evening light,
We gather in the heart's embrace.
From every corner, souls unite,
In love's unfathomable grace.

The bonds of spirit intertwine,
Through laughter, tears, and whispered prayer.
Divine connection, pure and fine,
In every heart, there dwells a share.

Together we walk this sacred path,
Each step a echo of ancient song.
We find our joy, we find our wrath,
In kinship, we forever belong.

When shadows cast their fleeting gloom,
Our light will shine through night's embrace.
In unity, we find our room,
To dwell in love's eternal space.

So let us sing of bonds divine,
With every heartbeat, echo loud.
In this communion, we align,
As one, united, joyful crowd.

Beneath the Starlit Veil of Unity

Beneath the stars, our chorus swells,
In whispered dreams, our spirits soar.
Each soul a story, every heart tells,
Of love that binds, forevermore.

The night enfolds us, soft and kind,
In cosmic dance, we lose all fear.
Within the stillness, peace we find,
A sacred space, we hold each dear.

The universe speaks in silent tones,
A language felt in every breath.
In harmony, our essence hones,
A bond communion that conquers death.

When shadows flicker, hope ignites,
With faith, we stand through tempest's rage.
Each heart a beacon, piercing nights,
Together we write a timeless page.

So let us gather, share this grace,
Underneath the starlit sky.
In every heart, a sacred place,
Where love and light will never die.

Through the Wounds of Division

In every fracture lies the chance,
To heal and find a greater whole.
Through every battle, every glance,
We seek to mend the broken soul.

When voices clash and tempers rise,
Let love be the balm for our pain.
In every tear and every sigh,
We strive to find the strength to gain.

The path may twist, the road may bend,
Yet in our hearts, we weave the thread.
For every wound, there lies a mend,
A chance for peace where love is spread.

Let not division claim its throne,
For in our hearts, a fire burns bright.
Together, we are never alone,
In unity, we find our light.

So let us stand hand in hand,
Through every trial, storm, or strife.
Within us flows a sacred strand,
Of love, of unity, of life.

A Remembrance of Sacred Wholeness

In every dawn, remember this,
A tapestry of souls entwined.
Through grace we find eternal bliss,
In every heart, a love defined.

The moments shared, the laughter bright,
Hold memories like treasures dear.
In sacred wholeness, lives the light,
A unity that conquers fear.

With every breath, let gratitude flow,
For every encounter, sacred space.
In every part, a greater glow,
In love's embrace, we find our place.

Through trials faced, the tears we shed,
We rise together, strong and bold.
In every word that's spoken, said,
A testament to stories told.

So celebrate the life we weave,
In every heart, a sacred trust.
In love and light, we must believe,
Together, in this path, we must.

The Revival of Belonging

In whispered prayers we gather here,
Hearts entwined, casting out fear.
A bond renewed under heaven's gaze,
Together we rise in sacred praise.

Through trials faced, we find our way,
Each step a truth, brightening the day.
Lost and found, we journey as one,
In unity's light, we are reborn.

Echoes of love guide our stride,
In the embrace of faith, we confide.
No soul alone in this embrace,
Together we seek the holy place.

With hands uplifted, we sing as one,
Grateful for battles fought and won.
In every heart, the light will show,
The revival of belonging, ever aglow.

Beneath the stars, we make our vow,
To cherish the moment, to live in now.
In laughter and tears, we affirm our stand,
United forever, in this promised land.

Sacred Memories of Kin

In the glow of twilight, stories unfold,
Of ancestors' strength and love untold.
Gathered around, the warmth we share,
In sacred memories, we find our prayer.

Roots run deep, history entwined,
A lineage rich, divinely designed.
Each tale a beacon, lighting the way,
Guiding our hearts as we kneel and pray.

Through seasons of change, our spirits align,
Echoes of laughter, forever divine.
In quiet moments, their voices we hear,
Sacred memories, ever so dear.

All generations, hand in hand,
Building a bridge to the promised land.
In every heartbeat, their love we trace,
A testament rich, to the holy grace.

So let us remember, together we thrive,
In the stories of kin, we feel alive.
Bound by faith and the ties unseen,
With sacred memories, we reign supreme.

The Whole Remains Within

In the stillness of prayer, we find our light,
The whole remains within, pure and bright.
Through trials and joy, our essence we see,
In the depth of silence, we learn to be free.

Whispers of hope echo in the soul,
Unseen yet felt, they make us whole.
A tapestry woven with threads of grace,
In the heart's quiet chamber, we embrace.

With faith as our guide, we venture afar,
In the darkest of nights, you're our guiding star.
In each humble moment, blessings begin,
For the whole remains within, deep within.

In every tear shed, in laughter and song,
We find our strength, where we all belong.
Connected in spirit, we rise and shine,
In this sacred truth, our hearts align.

So open your heart, let the journey unfold,
For the essence of life is a treasure untold.
In the embrace of love, let's journey within,
For the whole remains within, where it all begins.

The Pilgrimage of Us

Together we tread this sacred land,
In each step taken, we take a stand.
Hearts entwined amidst the strife,
On the pilgrimage of us, we weave our life.

Through valleys low and mountains high,
With hopes to carry, we reach for the sky.
In every challenge, we find our song,
On this path of faith, we grow strong.

With open arms, we share the grace,
In love's sweet embrace, we find our place.
Every road traveled, a lesson learned,
In the journey of us, our spirits burned.

With faith as our map and love as our guide,
We walk hand in hand, no need to hide.
For in unity's strength, we discover the truth,
On the pilgrimage of us, eternal proof.

Let the world witness our joyful stride,
In this holy journey, we walk with pride.
For in every heart, a flame does combust,
Together we venture, on the pilgrimage of us.

Reflections from the Mirror of Time

In silence, wisdom whispers low,
The past unfolds like drifting snow.
Each moment captured, softly shines,
A canvas etched with sacred signs.

As echoes of the heart arise,
We ponder truths beneath the skies.
In every tear, a lesson learned,
In every gaze, the soul discerned.

With gratitude, we trace the years,
Through valleys dark and joyous tears.
Each breath a prayer, a hymn of grace,
In this dance of time, we find our place.

The mirror shows both joy and pain,
Through shadows cast, we seek the gain.
In every trial, a seed is sown,
In every pathway, love is known.

So gather round, and share your light,
In unity, we rise from night.
With spirits bold, we'll forge ahead,
Reflections bright from all we've tread.

In the Garden of Our Shared Souls

In the garden where dreams take flight,
Each bloom a flame, a guiding light.
We walk together, hand in hand,
In sacred soil, where love is fanned.

Among the flowers, whispers weave,
Stories of hope that we believe.
In every petal, prayers take root,
In unity, our hearts commute.

The sun bestows its gentle grace,
On every seeker's yearning face.
With every drop of morning dew,
A promise blooms, forever true.

Beneath the stars, our spirits soar,
A symphony of souls, once more.
We'll dance upon this hallowed ground,
In love's embrace, true joy is found.

Let kindness grow, like vines entwined,
In this garden, hearts aligned.
Together we shall face the storms,
In faith and hope, our light transforms.

Remnants of a Blessed Communion

In sacred gatherings, spirits blend,
Moments cherished, love transcends.
Each word spoken, a thread divine,
Weaving souls as stars align.

With gratitude, we break the bread,
In every heart, His spirit spread.
Beneath the light of sacred grace,
We find communion in this space.

As echoes linger, shadows fade,
In every remnant, memories made.
A tapestry of life we share,
In every prayer, a bond laid bare.

Through trials faced, together bold,
The warmth of faith, a story told.
With hands united, visions gleam,
In love's embrace, we chase the dream.

So let us gather, hearts entwined,
In every soul, His love defined.
A legacy of hope we weave,
In blessed communion, we believe.

The Pilgrimage to Sacred Wholeness

With every step, a journey starts,
To sacred realms within our hearts.
In whispered dreams, we seek the way,
Through trials faced, we find the pay.

On winding paths, the seasons change,
In pain and joy, our lives arrange.
With courage held, we journey on,
For in each dusk, there comes the dawn.

In sacred silence, wisdom calls,
Reminding us that love befalls.
As we ascend the mountain high,
With open hearts, we touch the sky.

As pilgrims searched for truth and grace,
In every trial, we find our place.
Through every tear, a blessing grows,
In every heart, His presence flows.

So let us walk this path with peace,
In every step, our fears release.
Together we shall find the whole,
In love's embrace, we heal the soul.

Echoes of the Sacred Union

In the hush of dawn, souls entwine,
Bathed in the glow of starlit sign.
Hearts united in holy embrace,
Merging shadows in sacred space.

The sacred whispers through the trees,
Carrying prayers upon the breeze.
In unity's glow, spirits arise,
Reflecting truth in celestial skies.

Guided by love, we journey forth,
To the place of the eternal worth.
Every heartbeat a sacred call,
In the silence, we hear it all.

With every breath, the light ignites,
Illuminating the darkest nights.
Together we stand, hand in hand,
Bound by grace in this holy land.

Through trials faced, faith does lead,
In the garden of life, we plant the seed.
In echoes of love, we find our way,
Sacred union, forever we stay.

Fragments in the Light of Grace

In the stillness, glimmers appear,
Fragments of truth, gentle and clear.
Shattered pieces, yet whole within,
In grace's embrace, we begin again.

Each moment a brush with the divine,
Crafting the path where shadows align.
In the mosaic, our stories blend,
Through love's soft lens, we shall mend.

Broken wings learn to soar high,
Wisdom gathered in every sigh.
Through trials faced and rivers crossed,
In finding grace, we know no loss.

Light guides us through the darkest nights,
Filling our hearts with sacred sights.
In the fragments, we gather strength,
In love's embrace, we find our length.

Together we rise, united as one,
In the light of grace, we are reborn.
With each heartbeat, a promise made,
In the sacred dance, we are not afraid.

Whispers of Eternal Wholeness

In the quiet of dusk, whispers flow,
Echoes of love in the undertow.
Eternal waves on this sacred shore,
Remind us always of what we adore.

In every heartbeat, a tale unfolds,
Whispers of wholeness, gentle yet bold.
The tapestry woven in threads of grace,
Binding our spirits in divine embrace.

Lessons of life in the softest sighs,
In the stillness, our true essence lies.
Through every trial, our hearts align,
In whispers of unity, we find the divine.

With every step on this sacred ground,
The echoes of truth in silence resound.
In the dance of life, we freely flow,
Eternal wholeness in each of us grow.

Together we rise in love's sweet glow,
In unity's arms, we're destined to know.
Each whisper a promise, a sacred call,
In the embrace of the eternal, we stand tall.

The Journey Back to Eden

Upon the path where dreams reside,
We walk together, side by side.
The heart's desire calls us home,
In the garden of life, we freely roam.

Through archways of time, we seek the light,
Guided by love in the darkest night.
The whispers of wisdom, ever near,
Lead us back to where all is clear.

In every step, the pulse of grace,
We find the sacred in every space.
With open hearts, we embrace the dawn,
In the journey back, we are reborn.

Each twist and turn a lesson bestowed,
In the garden's arms, we share our load.
Bound by the spirit, together we tread,
In the light of creation, we're gently led.

The journey continues, love's endless song,
In the heart of Eden, we all belong.
With every breath, we shall become,
The essence of truth, eternally one.

Boundless in the Embrace of Faith

In the quiet dawn, we seek the light,
Hand in hand, we lift our sight.
A sacred bond, forever true,
In faith, we find our hearts renewed.

The whispers soft, they guide our way,
In every prayer, we humbly stay.
With open hearts, we share the grace,
In boundless love, we find our place.

Mountains rise, yet faith won't fade,
In trials deep, we are remade.
Each step we take, in trust we lean,
Together strong, we weave the unseen.

Through storms we journey, hand in hand,
In unity, we take our stand.
For in each moment, grace is sought,
In every silence, peace is taught.

Let love endure, let kindness reign,
In every heart, dissolve the pain.
With spirits bright, we lift our voice,
In faith, we find our true rejoice.

Interwoven Threads of the Divine

In the tapestry of life we weave,
Threads of love, we shall believe.
With every breath, a prayer ascends,
In unity, our spirit blends.

Moments shared, where hearts converge,
From silent cries, our souls emerge.
In joy's embrace, we weave the song,
Through trials faced, we're ever strong.

The divine spark within us glows,
In darkest nights, its brilliance shows.
With open minds, we search for truth,
In every heartbeat, find our youth.

Each morning light brings hope anew,
In gentle whispers, we hear you.
Through interwoven paths, we roam,
In faith's warm arms, we find our home.

Together we rise, hand in hand,
In every struggle, we understand.
For love's a thread, both strong and fine,
In the fabric of life, we intertwine.

Revelations of the Heart's Assembly

In the gathering light of dawn's embrace,
Hearts assemble, finding grace.
With open arms, we share our fears,
In love's connection, shed our tears.

In whispered prayers, our hopes take flight,
Together we stand, united in light.
In every glance, a story unfolds,
Of faith and trust, in hearts of gold.

Revelations bloom in gentle sighs,
In sacred moments, the spirit flies.
As storms may rage, we hold our ground,
In love's soft echo, strength is found.

Through trials faced and joy we share,
In every wound, a loving care.
With hands extended, we reach for peace,
In every bond, our souls release.

In the quiet night, we seek the light,
In solitude, our spirits ignite.
Revelations flow, a river wide,
In the heart's assembly, love's our guide.

In the Arms of Celestial Harmony

In twilight's glow, we find our path,
In stillness, feel the universe's wrath.
Yet in the chaos, a song takes flight,
In celestial harmony, we see the light.

With every breath, a moment shared,
In love's embrace, we are prepared.
Through whispers soft, the spirit calls,
In unity, we break down walls.

From every star, a promise shines,
In cosmic dance, our fate aligns.
In sacred spaces, we find release,
From earthly bounds, we seek our peace.

Together we rise, our voices blend,
In harmony's arms, we shall transcend.
With every heartbeat, faith anew,
In love's embrace, we start to view.

In the tapestry of night and day,
With every breath, we find our way.
For in each note, the truth will be,
In the arms of harmony, we are free.

The Tapestry of Our Common Spirit

Woven threads of grace unite,
Each soul a shining light.
In the fabric of our being,
We find the truth we're seeking.

In every heart, a sacred song,
In harmony, we all belong.
Together, we rise and claim,
The power of love in His name.

Through trials that we face each day,
Faith guides us along our way.
With every tear, a seed we plant,
In hope's embrace, we shall enchant.

The tapestry, so rich and bold,
A testament we weave of old.
Each color tells a tale and more,
Of unity forever to explore.

In silent prayers, our spirits soar,
In shared belief, we find the core.
Together bound by love's embrace,
In faith, we find our rightful place.

Reunited Under Heaven's Gaze

Beneath the stars, we come alive,
In faith's embrace, we shall survive.
Guided by light, we set our course,
Reunited, we feel love's force.

Through trials faced, we hold on tight,
With open hearts, we seek His light.
In every shadow, hope will bloom,
As faith dispels the deepest gloom.

Together, we journey hand in hand,
In sacred unity, we stand.
With every prayer, we touch the sky,
As hearts unite, we learn to fly.

Under His gaze, we find our way,
In love's embrace, darkness holds no sway.
With every breath, we sing His praise,
Eternal harmony displays.

We rise as one, a faithful choir,
In unity, we lift each other higher.
In spirit's dance, we bless the morn,
With hearts renewed, forever reborn.

Prayers from the Pulpit of the Past

In echoes soft, the ancients speak,
Their wisdom guides the humble, weak.
From shadows cast, their voices rise,
In reverent tone, they touch the skies.

Through sacred text, their truths unfold,
In every line, a tale retold.
With hearts alight, we seek to know,
The grace and love that they bestow.

In solemn prayer, we find our guide,
Through storms of life, they walk beside.
Each whispered vow, a sacred bond,
Through trials faced, we journey on.

Their love transcends the veil of time,
In every heart, their spirits chime.
With every prayer that we impart,
We feel their presence in our heart.

From pulpit high, the wisdom flows,
In timeless truths, we find repose.
With open arms, we hold the past,
In prayer, our souls are woven fast.

Echoes of the Forgotten Covenant

In whispers soft, a promise made,
In ancient times, it shall not fade.
Through valleys deep, the echoes call,
A covenant that binds us all.

Through storms and trials, we remember,
The fire of faith that burns like ember.
In every heart, a story waits,
Of love and grace that never abates.

Each step we take, a thread we weave,
In the fabric of what we believe.
United under the heavens bright,
We search for truth, we seek the light.

With every prayer, we find our way,
In His embrace, we long to stay.
Though shadows loom and doubts arise,
In faith's gentle hand, our spirit lies.

The echoes linger, guiding still,
In every heart, a sacred will.
With joy and love, we stand as one,
In gratitude, our souls have won.

Threads of Light in the Weaving Dark

In shadows thick, where silence dwells,
The threads of faith, a story tells.
Upon the loom, divine hands weave,
A tapestry of hope, we believe.

Each strand a prayer, each knot a bond,
In every heart, the light responds.
Though darkness looms, it cannot sever,
The ties of love that last forever.

Through trials faced, and burdens shared,
In every moment, God has cared.
With each new dawn, the colors blaze,
A symphony of joy and praise.

In woven patterns, life unfolds,
In whispered truths, the story holds.
Together strong, we brave the night,
With threads of light, we find our sight.

So hold your faith, let courage rise,
In darkest hours, behold the skies.
For in the weaving, we are found,
Threads of light, forever bound.

The Blessing of Togetherness in Solitude

In quiet moments, we discover grace,
A sacred space, where hearts embrace.
In solitude, the spirit sings,
A blessing found in silent things.

Though alone we face the trials near,
In stillness soft, love's voice we hear.
With every breath, a bond is grown,
In sacred silence, we're not alone.

In whispered prayers, our souls entwine,
The strength of many, a holy sign.
In solitude, together we stand,
United still, by faith's command.

For in the stillness, blessings gleam,
In every thought, a shared dream.
Together in spirit, though apart in pain,
The heart's connection forever remains.

So cherish moments where silence reigns,
In solitude, our love remains.
Through distance felt, we find our way,
In togetherness, we choose to stay.

From the Ashes of Disconnection

From fragments lost, we rise anew,
In faith's embrace, we find what's true.
Ashes fall, the fire dims,
Yet hope ignites, within our hymns.

In brokenness, the heart still beats,
A symphony of love repeats.
From depths of sorrow, we shall soar,
Embracing light, forevermore.

The path was dark, the road unclear,
Yet in our trials, we persevere.
With every step, we claim our song,
From ashes gray, we will be strong.

Together forged, through pain refined,
A sense of purpose, we will find.
In unity, our spirits blend,
From shattered past, new paths we'll wend.

So rise up, dear souls, and take your flight,
From the ashes, we reclaim our light.
With open hearts, we kindle the flame,
In love's embrace, we'll never be the same.

A Testament of Hearts Rejoined

In distant lands, where hearts once cried,
A testament of love, we abide.
Through every storm, together we stand,
In faith's embrace, we join our hands.

Each tear we've shed, a seed of grace,
In trials faced, we find our place.
The journey long, yet spirits soar,
A union blessed, forevermore.

We gather strength from tales we share,
In every memory, we declare:
The bonds we forge, though time may test,
In love's embrace, we find our rest.

With every heartbeat, we renew,
A testament of trust, so true.
In every laugh, in every sigh,
Our hearts rejoined, a sacred tie.

So let us walk this road with pride,
In unity, we shall abide.
For every step brings love's sweet song,
A testament of hearts grown strong.

The Parable of Lost Unity

In a garden of faith, we stood,
Hand in hand, as brothers we could.
Yet shadows fell upon our hearts,
Torn apart, where silence starts.

The words of wisdom left unsaid,
Broke the bond that once had led.
In whispers lost to the night,
We searched for hope, for guiding light.

Each step we take on winding ways,
Echoes of love in lost arrays.
Where are the vows we once did pledge?
Faded now on life's sharp edge.

Yet still the dawn will break anew,
With gentle grace, a chance for two.
To mend the seams of unity,
And live as one in harmony.

So lift your eyes beyond the strife,
For peace is found in shared life.
In every heart, a song can rise,
Together, we will touch the skies.

The Pilgrim's Path to Equanimity

With each step upon this road,
A journey shared, a blessed ode.
In every trial, a chance to glow,
Through valleys deep, to mountains' snow.

The burdened mind seeks calmness here,
In prayerful thoughts, we draw near.
With every breath, let worries cease,
In faith we find our truest peace.

The sun will rise with burning grace,
Guiding pilgrims in this space.
Through storms and trials, we learn to bend,
Trusting that love will never end.

Together we shall cross the hills,
Embracing all the heart fulfills.
In patience, hope will softly bloom,
A sacred light dispelling gloom.

So walk with me and hand in hand,
In unity, together we stand.
For every step, a prayer we weave,
On this path, our souls believe.

Celestial Bonds of Yesterday

In whispers of the stars above,
We find the echoes of lost love.
Each memory a thread so fine,
Woven through the hands of time.

The moon reflects our ancient plight,
Guiding hearts through darkest night.
Though ages pass, the spark remains,
In silent songs, where peace sustains.

The tapestry of days long gone,
Speaks of Unity, softly drawn.
In every fiber, a golden chance,
To reunite in sacred dance.

With every dawn, a chance to see,
The bonds that tie you back to me.
In realms of love, we shall reclaim,
The joy that blooms within our names.

So let us honor what was shared,
In memories, we find we cared.
For in the stars and skies up high,
Celestial bonds can never die.

Harmony in the Temple of Us

Within the walls of sacred space,
Where love abounds, we find our grace.
In the temple of each heart, we meet,
In gentle whispers, our souls greet.

The candles glow with fervent flame,
Each flicker speaks a shared name.
In unity, we raise our song,
Together, where we all belong.

The incense swirls, a fragrant prayer,
Reaching high, we breathe the air.
Through trials faced, we stand as one,
In harmony, our fears undone.

The altar holds our hopes so dear,
In tender moments, we draw near.
With open hearts and spirits free,
We nurture love, a sacred tree.

So let us sing within this room,
With voices raised, dispelling gloom.
In the temple where our hearts unite,
We find our peace, our shared light.

Every Shattered Piece a Prayer

In the stillness of the night, we weep,
Each fragment of hope laid down at His feet.
Broken spirits soar like doves in flight,
Whispers of love that no pain can defeat.

Every tear a testament to our plea,
He gathers them gently, with hands that heal.
In our sorrow, we find the key,
Through shattered pieces, His grace we feel.

Once lost in shadows, now we arise,
With faith restored, we seek the light.
Every wound a story, every scar a prize,
In God's embrace, there's infinite might.

In the tapestry of trials, we weave,
A chorus of hearts entwined through strife.
Here in His love, we learn to believe,
Every shattered piece, a prayer for life.

So let us gather, hand in hand, we stand,
Shouting praises that echo 'round.
In unity's strength, we form a band,
Every shattered piece, by faith, unbound.

Testament of the Interwoven Hearts

Threads of compassion, woven with care,
Hearts entwined in a sacred embrace.
With each heartbeat, a promise we share,
In the tapestry of love, we find our place.

Through trials faced, our spirits unite,
Every joy and sorrow, a dance in grace.
Connected by faith, we rise in the light,
A testament to hope, time cannot erase.

With whispered prayers, we birth new dreams,
In every moment, His mercy flows free.
In harmony's song, our souls find their themes,
Together, forever, in sweet unity.

All struggles fall away at His feet,
In sacred silence, our hearts find their tune.
As one, we rise, our mission complete,
Interwoven, we shine, like stars and the moon.

Let us gather the fragments, stitch them with care,
A quilt of our stories, rich and profound.
In love's gentle arms, nothing can tear,
This testament of hearts, forever bound.

The Altar of Longing

At the altar, we lay our dreams bare,
Crying out to the heavens above.
In the silent whispers, God hears our prayer,
Longing for peace, for mercy, for love.

With every ache, a heart learns to know,
That through desperation, salvation is sown.
In faith's sacred journey, our spirits will grow,
Each longing ignites a flame brightly shown.

In waiting, we find a strength so divine,
Our hopes woven tightly, like vines on a tree.
He opens the doors of His heart, not a sign,
For every intention, He holds the key.

We gather the sorrows, wrapped tight in His grace,
Each burden released, a step toward the dawn.
At this altar of longing, we find our place,
Where faith is reborn, and fear is withdrawn.

Our cries become hymns, a melody bright,
For the love that endures, the heart cannot hide.
In unity's strength, we claim our birthright,
At the altar of longing, where hope is our guide.

A Cantata for the Divided

In shadows we linger, hearts split apart,
Yet within us resides a hope that ignites.
With melodies rising, we seek to impart,
A cantata for all, uniting our flights.

With voices like rivers, we flow toward the sea,
Bridges of harmony, crossing wide gaps.
In this great symphony, let there be peace,
For love has the power to close all the laps.

Though paths may diverge, each step holds a prize,
In the music of life, we find our true song.
With faith as our compass, we'll reach for the skies,
And no note of discord shall linger for long.

Let the rhythms of kindness break through the chains,
And the chords of forgiveness resound through the night.
For hearts intertwined, though there may be pains,
Together we flourish, in love, we find light.

So here's to the journey, let's rise as one voice,
In this cantata for souls, divided yet whole.
Amidst the chaos, let our hearts rejoice,
For we are the music, the spirit, the soul.

The Relics of Our Spirit

In sacred silence, whispers dwell,
Eternal truths, we yearn to tell.
Through trials faced, our hearts unfold,
In cherished warmth, our stories told.

With every prayer, our spirits rise,
Like incense lifted to the skies.
The relics grace, both near and far,
In unity, we find our star.

From shadows cast, the light breaks through,
A guiding flame, forever true.
As echoes fade in evening's calm,
We seek the peace, we find the balm.

In every laugh, a holy hymn,
In every tear, a love within.
Together we tread this sacred ground,
In faith, our purpose is profound.

With open hearts, we greet the dawn,
In harmony, our spirits drawn.
For every soul that joins the quest,
In love and light, we find our rest.

In the Light of Shared Souls

Under the heavens, our spirits merge,
In the soft glow, our hearts converge.
Each path we walk, a testament,
To bonds that stretch, to life well spent.

In laughter shared and tears that flow,
Through every storm, our spirits grow.
Together we lift, together we sing,
In the light of love, our souls take wing.

A tapestry woven, each thread divine,
In every heartbeat, our fates entwined.
In sacred moments, we find our place,
In harmony's hold, we know His grace.

From every shadow, we seek the light,
In the warmth of faith, banishing night.
Our echoes dance on the winds of prayer,
In shared souls' embrace, we find repair.

With every dawn, we rise anew,
In the vast expanse, our spirits flew.
In unity's glow, our hearts ignite,
In love's embrace, we find our sight.

Seraphic Fragments

From heaven's realm, the fragments fall,
A dance of light, a sacred call.
Each shard reflects a truth so pure,
In every heart, a love that's sure.

Through trials faced, a beauty borne,
In the midst of night, we greet the morn.
The wings of grace, around us sweep,
In divine presence, our souls keep.

A symphony of whispers soft,
Revealing gifts that lift us oft.
In humble prayer, we find our song,
In seraphic fragments, we belong.

Each fleeting moment, a glimpse divine,
Each breath a chance to intertwine.
In love's embrace, we rise and soar,
In seraphic grace, forever more.

With faith as our anchor, we journey on,
Through every dusk, into each dawn.
In the light of love, forever free,
In seraphic fragments, we shall be.

Unity's Lasting Embrace

In the arms of love, we gather near,
With open hearts, casting out fear.
In every smile, a blessing flows,
In unity's warmth, our spirit glows.

Through every valley, our strength we find,
In moments shared, our souls aligned.
A bond unbroken, a sacred thread,
In unity's fold, we are gently led.

In acts of kindness, we plant the seeds,
Of love and hope, our hearts' true needs.
In every prayer, a promise made,
In unity's grace, we shall not fade.

With every heartbeat, we stand as one,
Through every trial, until it's done.
In the light of truth, we find our way,
In unity's embrace, we choose to stay.

For in each moment, a chance to love,
Uniting souls, as stars above.
In the sacred bond, we rise above,
In unity's song, our hearts will shove.

Meditations on the Ties that Bind

In silence we gather, hearts entwined,
A thread of grace in the vast design.
With faith as our anchor, we journey wide,
In unity's embrace, we shall abide.

Through trials we walk, hand in hand,
Faithful as the tides that kiss the sand.
In sacred whispers, our spirits soar,
Bound by love's light, forevermore.

The bonds we nurture in shadows and sun,
In every heartbeat, we're forever one.
Each laugh, each tear, a testament true,
To the holy ties that bind me to you.

As seasons shift and time does wane,
In moments of joy, in sorrow's strain,
United we stand, through shifting sands,
In the peace that comes from love's gentle hands.

With every prayer, a thread is spun,
From soul to soul, we are all as one.
In the tapestry woven, we find our place,
Meditations on the love we embrace.

In Search of the Sanctuary of Togetherness

In the quiet woods where whispers dwell,
We seek the heart of our sacred shell.
Beneath the boughs, in nature's care,
The sanctuary calls, a promise rare.

With every step, the spirit sings,
Of love's embrace and the hope it brings.
Among the trees, in the soft, warm light,
Together we find our souls unite.

The gentle breeze, a soft caress,
Inviting us into a world of blessed rest.
We share our dreams in the golden glade,
In trust and truth, our fears do fade.

As the sun descends, our shadows blend,
In the peaceful hour, hearts mend.
The warmth of togetherness shines so bright,
In the sanctuary of love, we take flight.

Hand in hand, we redefine,
The essence of being, so divine.
In the timeless dance of the eternal now,
We honor the connection, here and how.

The Traces of Our Divine Kinship

In every glance, a spark ignites,
The traces of love in shared delights.
With every breath, we weave our fate,
In the light of kinship, love radiates.

Through trials faced, our spirits merge,
In the bond of faith, we find the surge.
Each heartbeat echoes a sacred song,
In the arms of Heaven, we all belong.

As stars align in the velvet night,
We trace the path to eternal light.
The memories linger, sweet and strong,
Of joyous laughter and nights so long.

In silence shared or spoken word,
The language of love is deeply heard.
Our souls entwined, a dance divine,
With every step, the grace we find.

Across the heavens, our spirits soar,
In the kinship's embrace, forevermore.
A testament true to the bonds we share,
In every heartbeat, there you are, there!

Faith Unbroken by Time's Tide

In the rush of life and the pull of time,
Faith stands strong, an endless climb.
Through storms that rage and skies that clear,
We find our footing, free from fear.

In every challenge, our spirits rise,
With courage enshrined in Heaven's eyes.
Across the valleys, through the strife,
Our faith unbroken, the essence of life.

Like rivers flowing, we ebb and swell,
In the sacred dance, we know it well.
Each moment cherished, a gift bestowed,
In the heart's soft whisper, love is owed.

Through passage of time, we hold the light,
A beacon of hope in the darkest night.
In the arms of love, we find our guide,
Faith unbroken by time's relentless tide.

Together we stand, against the years,
With prayers of joy and uncried tears.
In the tapestry of life, brightly we weave,
Faith everlasting, in dreams we believe.

Incandescent Memories of Us

In twilight's glow, our spirits meld,
Whispers of love, secrets held.
In sacred spaces, where we dwell,
Echoes of laughter, like a spell.

Touched by grace, our hearts align,
In every moment, a sign divine.
Together we dance, in time's embrace,
Guided by light, we find our place.

Through trials faced, our faith ignites,
In shadows deep, we seek the lights.
In every tear, a lesson learned,
With every breath, our passion burned.

With open arms, we walk the path,
In silent prayers, we find our wrath.
For in each promise, a truth unfolds,
An incandescent warmth that never grows old.

Prayers from the Fractured

In broken whispers, our hopes collide,
Among the ruins, we choose to abide.
Each scar a story, a path we've crossed,
In prayerful silence, we count the cost.

With humble hearts, we bow our heads,
For every wound, a love that spreads.
In the cracks of despair, we find the light,
A flicker of faith, shining so bright.

From the depths of sorrow, we rise anew,
In the arms of mercy, a love so true.
With every tear, a seed is sown,
A prayer ensuing, we're never alone.

So here we gather, in hope and grace,
Finding strength in this sacred space.
Through fractured prayers, our voices blend,
A melody tender, that will not end.

Mosaic of the Divine Heart

In every shard, a story glows,
Colors of faith in the beauty flows.
Together we weave, a tapestry bright,
In the mosaic of love, we find our light.

Pieces scattered, yet intertwined,
In sacred union, our spirits aligned.
With every heartbeat, a vibration true,
In the divine heart, we are born anew.

Fragile yet bold, this art we create,
In moments of joy, we celebrate.
Each fragment a lesson, a divine embrace,
In the mosaic of life, we find our place.

So with open hands, we share our souls,
In the dance of the spirit, we play our roles.
Together we shine, a harmony pure,
In the mosaic of love, forever secure.

Resounding Echoes of Unity

In silent chambers, our hearts unite,
Resounding echoes in the tranquil night.
Through whispered prayers, we seek the truth,
In this sacred bond, we find our youth.

Each voice a note in the symphony grand,
Together we rise, hand in hand.
Across the valleys, our spirits soar,
Resounding echoes, forevermore.

In laughter and tears, in love we dwell,
In harmony's promise, all is well.
With every breath, we weave the song,
In unity's embrace, we all belong.

So let us gather, with hope ablaze,
In the echoes of love, we sing our praise.
For in each heartbeat, a truth unfolds,
Resounding whispers of love retold.

The Holy Assembly of Memory

In shadows cast by ancient light,
We gather souls to seek the bright.
Each whisper holds a sacred creed,
In silence, hearts and spirits heed.

The tapestry of ages spun,
With threads of hope, we come as one.
Together, woven stories rise,
Each moment shared, a sweet surprise.

With hands uplifted, prayers unfold,
In every breath, a truth retold.
Across the years, we pave the way,
In joyous hymns, we wish to stay.

The echoes call from deep within,
As memories dance, our souls begin.
In sacred halls where whispers flow,
The seeds of love and faith will grow.

So let us stand, our hearts aligned,
In reverence, all spirits bind.
For in this holy assembly, we find,
The strength of love, forever kind.

Sacred Symphonies of Us

In harmony, our voices rise,
A chorus sung beneath the skies.
Each note a prayer, a gentle sigh,
Connecting hearts, we soar and fly.

The melodies of time resound,
In unity, our souls are found.
With every beat, we intertwine,
In sacred love, our spirits shine.

Through trials faced, we hold in trust,
In symphonies, we blend the dust.
Together, we shall stand so tall,
With every step, we hear the call.

Embracing dreams that light the way,
We sing of peace, a brighter day.
In every heart, a sacred song,
In this communion, we belong.

So let us play this life, it's true,
In rhythms old and visions new.
Together weaving tales divine,
In sacred symphonies, we shine.

Echoes from the Sacred Grove

In stillness found beneath the trees,
The whispers dance upon the breeze.
Each rustle speaks of ancient lore,
As spirits linger evermore.

The branches weave a sacred thread,
Where hearts once lost are gently led.
We walk among the silent stones,
In nature's peace, we find our home.

The echoes linger, soft and clear,
In every sigh, a chant, a cheer.
With roots that ground us deep and wide,
We find the strength to turn the tide.

In every leaf, a prayerful grace,
Divine connections we embrace.
With open hearts, we share the glow,
As love and light from nature flow.

So let us gather, hand in hand,
In sacred spaces, we will stand.
For in this grove, our spirits blend,
In echoes lush, our souls ascend.

Beneath the Canopy of Togetherness

Beneath the branches, wide and green,
We come together, hearts serene.
In unity, a bond so dear,
With every laugh, we cast out fear.

The sky above, a tapestry,
Of dreams that soar with clarity.
With every hug, a shared embrace,
In this safe haven, find our place.

Through storms that come and trials faced,
In love's warm light, we find our grace.
With stories shared and hands entwined,
In every moment, peace we find.

So let us dance beneath this dome,
In laughter, joy, we find our home.
For in this space of sweet delight,
Together, we shine ever bright.

In whispers soft, our prayers ascend,
In gratitude, on love we depend.
Beneath this canopy, we know,
In togetherness, our spirits grow.

The Alpha of Our Togetherness

In the dawn of faith we gather near,
Voices blend, casting out all fear.
Hearts entwined, a sacred thread,
In the light of love, we daily tread.

Together we rise, as one, we stand,
In grace we find a guiding hand.
Each prayer a beacon, softly shared,
In unity's embrace, we are declared.

Through trials faced and storms we weather,
Faith unites us, binding tether.
In the chorus of souls, a vibrant sound,
The Alpha calls, in joy we're found.

With each step forward, we honor the past,
Holding together, our bond is steadfast.
In the melody of life, we sing our plea,
The gift of togetherness, eternally free.

In the tapestry woven, thread by thread,
With love and compassion, our spirits are fed.
Under heaven's watch, we journey, we roam,
In the heart of the world, we'll always find home.

Celestial Notes of a Lost Symphony

In the silence, echoes of grace,
A melody lost, seeking its place.
Stars above weave a tale so bright,
In the darkness, we grasp for light.

Notes of longing drift through the skies,
In whispered prayers, our spirits rise.
Celestial echoes fill the night air,
In this symphony, we find our share.

Each heartbeat a rhythm, divine and true,
Connecting the heavens to me and you.
With every breath, let the music flow,
In resonant waves, together we grow.

Through the valleys of doubt, where shadows play,
The harmony calls, lighting the way.
In the quiet of night, we listen and learn,
For celestial notes, within us, burn.

As we seek the melody lost to time,
In faith's embrace, we softly climb.
With each step taken, a song is reborn,
In the heart of togetherness, a new dawn is worn.

Hymns of Unity and Reverence

In unity's name, we gather as one,
With reverence deep, our hearts have begun.
Each word a prayer, each note a plea,
In the light of love, we find our key.

Through trials faced, hands held in trust,
In the sacred bond, we live, we must.
Voices lifted, a choir so pure,
In harmony's grace, our spirits endure.

In the silence, our souls intertwine,
With faith we walk, on this path divine.
Every heartbeat sings of the truth we embrace,
In the hymns of our lives, we find our place.

With reverent hearts, we light the way,
Guiding each other, come what may.
In the embrace of the divine, we belong,
Together we rise, together we're strong.

In the tapestry woven through prayer and song,
We journey together, where we all belong.
In the unity of faith, hand in hand we stand,
Hymns of love echo across this land.

The Unbroken Circle of Belonging

In the circle of life, we gather anew,
Each soul a light, shining through.
An unbroken bond, woven in time,
In the forge of belonging, we find our rhyme.

With open hearts, we share our dreams,
In kindness found, love brightly beams.
The stories we carry, rich and wide,
In the circle of faith, there is no divide.

With each gentle word, we foster peace,
In the warmth of togetherness, we find release.
A tapestry crafted of hope and grace,
In belonging's embrace, we find our place.

As seasons change, our roots go deep,
In the garden of love, we sow and reap.
Together we rise, in trust we stand,
An unbroken circle, hand in hand.

In the heart of our circle, let love prevail,
In every whisper, we tell the tale.
For in belonging, we find our strength,
In this circle of life, we find our length.

The Covenant of Sacred Wholeness

In the silence of the dawn, we stand,
Bound by promises, sweet and grand.
Hearts align beneath the skies,
In unity, our spirit flies.

Woven threads of grace and love,
Guided by the light above.
Each soul a piece, a star so bright,
Together shining, day and night.

Through trials faced and battles fought,
In sacred wholeness, we are taught.
From brokenness, we find our way,
In harmony, we rise and sway.

A covenant made in sacred trust,
In every heart, a holy gust.
To cherish peace, to seek the right,
In boundless joy, our spirits light.

Forever joined, we walk the path,
In quiet strength, we quell the wrath.
With open arms and open hearts,
We gather love, as truth imparts.

Glimmers of a Shared Past

We gather here beneath the tree,
Where stories whisper wild and free.
Fingers trace the lines of fate,
A dance of time we celebrate.

In sacred fires, our voices blend,
Echoes of the past transcend.
Memories woven, thread by thread,
In humble grace, our hearts are led.

Through trials faced and laughter shared,
In every burden, love declared.
Glimmers shine through darkest nights,
Our shared past ignites the lights.

With every song, our spirits rise,
In unity, we touch the skies.
Together, we embrace our truth,
In reverence for forgotten youth.

As dawn breaks wide, we find our way,
To honor bonds that will not sway.
In every heart, a story glows,
From shared past, our spirit flows.

Psalms of the Seamless Spirit

In melodies of gentle grace,
We lift our hearts, our sacred place.
Psalms arise like morning dew,
Binding us to all that's true.

Each note a prayer, each word a light,
Guiding us through the darkest night.
In seamless spirit, we unite,
Resilience born from love's pure sight.

Through valleys deep and mountains high,
Our voices soar, a sweet reply.
In silent moments, wisdom grows,
The spirit's path, forever flows.

With every verse, our hopes are sung,
In harmony, our souls are strung.
Together, we embrace the whole,
In psalms of love, we find our role.

As waves of time crash on the shore,
We sing of peace, forevermore.
In every heartbeat, every tear,
The seamless spirit draws us near.

The Gathering of Exiled Voices

From distant lands, we come to share,
Our stories woven in the air.
Exiled hearts, yet never lost,
In every soul, we bear the cost.

Voices rising, strong and clear,
In unity, we conquer fear.
The gathering, a sacred space,
Where love and hope will interlace.

Through struggle's test, our spirits lend,
A hand to those who need a friend.
In every whisper, strength is found,
Together, we stand on sacred ground.

From ashes grown, our dreams ignite,
In fervent love, we dare to fight.
A chorus built on bonds of trust,
In every heart, there's sacred dust.

With lifted voices, we create,
A world renewed, we celebrate.
Exiled no more, we find our way,
In this gathering, come what may.

The Light That Held Us

In darkness fell, we sought the flame,
A light that whispers love's sweet name.
Together we rise, hands interlace,
Guided by grace in this sacred space.

The lanterns of hope shone ever bright,
Illuminating paths in the night.
In every heart, a spark ignites,
Uniting souls in love's pure sights.

Through trials faced, we stand as one,
Our spirits woven, never undone.
With every prayer, our voices blend,
A chorus strong, on God we depend.

In gentle winds, our hearts take flight,
Through every storm, we seek the light.
The bonds we form, a testament true,
In love, we trust, our faith renewed.

So let us shine, let love transpire,
In every heart, ignite the fire.
Together we journey, hand in hand,
In the light that held us, we boldly stand.

Chronicles of the Unified Spirit

In pages worn, our stories dwell,
Tales of love, of hope, we tell.
Through trials faced, each chapter shared,
The strength of unity, forever paired.

As rivers flow, our hearts entwined,
A tapestry woven, forever aligned.
In every struggle, in every song,
Together we rise, steadfast and strong.

Voices echo in the sacred night,
Guided by faith, by divine light.
Each step we take, a journey blessed,
A path of love, our souls at rest.

In laughter shared, in sorrows healed,
The power of love is there revealed.
With open hearts, we lift our gaze,
To the unified spirit, we give praise.

So let our story continue to flow,
In every heart, let unity grow.
With each page turned, let love inspire,
Chronicles of the spirit, a sacred fire.

Paschal Pathways to Togetherness

On pathways bright, we search for grace,
Through every trial, we find our place.
With hope in hearts, we walk as one,
In the light of love, our journey begun.

The whispers of faith guide every step,
Through shadows deep, our souls adept.
In moments shared, in laughter and tears,
Together bound, we conquer fears.

Paschal blessings, in each embrace,
Uniting spirits in a sacred space.
With every heartbeat, our love extends,
The pathways of grace, where joy transcends.

As dawn awakens the night's soft song,
We lift our voices, together strong.
In unity's dance, we find our true joy,
The peace of togetherness, none can destroy.

So let us walk on this sacred path,
Guided by love, through the aftermath.
In every moment, let kindness unfold,
Paschal pathways, where hearts turn to gold.

The Divine Song of Kinship

In every heart, a melody sings,
Echoes of love on angel's wings.
The harmony found in kinship's embrace,
Unites our joys, our trials, our grace.

With every note, a story is spun,
The dance of our lives forever begun.
In laughter shared and tears released,
The divine song brings us to peace.

Through endless nights and sunlit days,
In gratitude, we lift our praise.
For every voice, in chorus we rise,
The song of kinship beneath the skies.

Let love be the tether, the sacred thread,
Binding us close, where angels tread.
In every heartbeat, in every sigh,
The divine song of kinship will fly.

So let us sing with a joyous heart,
For in this song, we'll never part.
Together forever, in love's sweet throng,
We celebrate life with the divine song.

The Divine Mosaic of Us

In the tapestry of light, we weave,
Each thread a whispered prayer believed.
Together we rise, hands intertwined,
In unity's grace, our souls aligned.

Colors of faith blend, vibrant and bright,
A mosaic of hearts, reflecting the light.
In the sacred bond, our spirits engage,
With love as the ink, we write our page.

Through trials we shine, each fracture a spark,
Resilient in purpose, igniting the dark.
Each piece a story, a witness of strife,
In the art of existence, we celebrate life.

As mountains stand tall, unwavering, strong,
In the symphony of hope, we sing our song.
A vision of peace, a dance of the free,
In this divine journey, we're meant to be.

So let us embrace the mosaic we form,
With kindness as compass, through every storm.
In the blend of our hearts, we find our way,
Together we flourish, come what may.

Pilgrimage of the Together

We wander through valleys where shadows reside,
With faith as our lantern, we walk side by side.
Each step a reminder of journeys unknown,
In the pilgrimage sacred, love is our own.

Mountains we climb with hearts open wide,
In the breath of the earth, our spirits confide.
Through rivers of sorrow, we find our flow,
In the quilt of existence, together we grow.

With echoes of prayers beneath starlit skies,
We gather our dreams, where the limitless lies.
In memories woven, our stories unfold,
The paths that we travel, in truth, we behold.

Courage our compass, we journey in grace,
In the warmth of compassion, we find our place.
No distance too great, if hearts intertwine,
In the trust of each other, our dreams align.

So let us walk onward, with purpose anew,
In the pilgrimage shared, we renew our view.
Together in spirit, united we roam,
Finding in each other, our everlasting home.

Celestial Communion

In the fabric of night, we quietly dwell,
With stars as our witness, we share and we tell.
The whispers of angels, a soft serenade,
In celestial communion, together we wade.

Each heartbeat a rhythm, syncing divine,
In the silence of space, our spirits align.
The cosmos around us, a symphony vast,
With every shared moment, true bonds are cast.

Through seasons of change, we bow to the dance,
In the light of each other, we find our chance.
With hope as our guide, we float on the breeze,
In communion so holy, we're brought to our knees.

As we gather in love, like fireflies aglow,
Our essence ignited, the spirit will grow.
In the warmth of a smile, we gather the light,
In celestial embrace, all wrongs turn to right.

Together we rise, like the dawn after night,
In this sacred connection, our souls take flight.
Eternal the bond, in the heavens above,
In celestial communion, we are wrapped in love.

Refuge of Remembered Love

In the quiet of dusk, where dreams gently fold,
We find the retreat that the heart has foretold.
In the refuge of memories, tender and warm,
We gather the fragments, and cradle the calm.

Each moment a treasure, a soft, whispered tune,
In the garden of shadows, we dance with the moon.
With petals of laughter, our sorrows we share,
In the fold of remembered love, we lay bare.

Time weaves its magic, through joy and through pain,
In the shelter of kindness, we rise once again.
In the tapestry woven, our stories entwine,
In the refuge of love, forever we shine.

As the seasons shift, and the echoes remain,
In the heart's quiet chamber, we're free of disdain.
Through the corridors of time, together we stand,
In the refuge of love, forever hand in hand.

So let us remember, as shadows may play,
In the warmth of each other, we find our way.
In the refuge of love, our spirits renew,
Together forever, our bond tried and true.